FINESSING OVER MY FINANCES PLANNER

DAMIAYA ROBINSON

BILL PAYMENT TRACKER

BILL	DATE	$	JA	FB	MR	AP	MY	JN	JL	AG	SP	OC	NV	DE

SAVINGS TRACKER

FOR:	AMOUNT NEEDED:

DUE DATE	PLANNED	SAVED	STILL TO BE SAVED

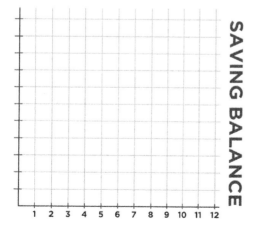

SAVING BALANCE

1 2 3 4 5 6 7 8 9 10 11 12

NOTES

MONTHLY BILLS

MONTH:	BUDGET GOAL:

INCOME

DATE	DESCRIPTION	AMOUNT	AFTER TAX

FIXED EXPENSES			OTHER EXPENSES		
DATE	DESCRIPTION	AMOUNT	DATE	DESCRIPTION	AMOUNT

	BUDGETED	ACTUAL	DIFFERENCE
TOTAL EXPENSES			
TOTAL INCOME			
TOTAL SAVINGS			

DEBT PAYMENT TRACKER

| DEBT: | CREDITOR: | PAYMENT DATE: |

STARTING BALANCE: _____ **ACCOUNT:** _____

JANUARY	FEBRUARY	MARCH	APRIL	MAY	JUNE

JULY	AUGUST	SEPTEMBER	OCTOBER	NOVEMBER	DECEMBER

ENDING BALANCE: _____

| DEBT: | CREDITOR: | PAYMENT DATE: |

STARTING BALANCE: _____ **ACCOUNT:** _____

JANUARY	FEBRUARY	MARCH	APRIL	MAY	JUNE

JULY	AUGUST	SEPTEMBER	OCTOBER	NOVEMBER	DECEMBER

ENDING BALANCE: _____

| DEBT: | CREDITOR: | PAYMENT DATE: |

STARTING BALANCE: _____ **ACCOUNT:** _____

JANUARY	FEBRUARY	MARCH	APRIL	MAY	JUNE

JULY	AUGUST	SEPTEMBER	OCTOBER	NOVEMBER	DECEMBER

ENDING BALANCE: _____

MONTHLY BUDGET

ITEM	BUDGET	ACTUAL	DIFFERENCE	NOTES
CATEGORY:				
CATEGORY:				
CATEGORY:				
CATEGORY:				
CATEGORY:				

EXPENSE TRACKER

DATE	DESCRIPTION	INCOME	OUTGOING

TOTAL INCOME:	TOTAL OUTGOINGS:	BALANCE:

ACCOUNT DETAILS

ACCOUNT:

STARTING BALANCE:

DATE	TRANSACTION	WITHDRAWAL	DEPOSIT	BALANCE

NOTES

WEEKLY EXPENSES

ITEM	BUDGETED	ACTUAL	DIFFERENCE	DUE DATE	PAID
WEEK 1					

SAVINGS [_____] **LEFTOVER** [_____]

ITEM	BUDGETED	ACTUAL	DIFFERENCE	DUE DATE	PAID
WEEK 2					

SAVINGS [_____] **LEFTOVER** [_____]

WEEKLY EXPENSES

ITEM	BUDGETED	ACTUAL	DIFFERENCE	DUE DATE	PAID
WEEK 3					

SAVINGS [   ]   **LEFTOVER** [   ]

ITEM	BUDGETED	ACTUAL	DIFFERENCE	DUE DATE	PAID
WEEK 4					

SAVINGS [   ]   **LEFTOVER** [   ]

MONTH: _____

TO DO LIST:

NOTES:

DAILY

DATE   __/__/____   FOCUS

TO DO

- ○ _____
- ○ _____
- ○ _____
- ○ _____
- ○ _____
- ○ _____
- ○ _____
- ○ _____
- ○ _____
- ○ _____

APPOINTMENTS-CALLS

NOTES

DAILY

DATE   __/__/____   FOCUS

quote

TO DO

- ○ _____
- ○ _____
- ○ _____
- ○ _____
- ○ _____
- ○ _____
- ○ _____
- ○ _____
- ○ _____
- ○ _____

APPOINTMENTS-CALLS

NOTES

DAILY

DATE __/__/____   FOCUS

quote

TO DO

- ○ _____
- ○ _____
- ○ _____
- ○ _____
- ○ _____
- ○ _____
- ○ _____
- ○ _____
- ○ _____
- ○ _____

APPOINTMENTS-CALLS

NOTES

DAILY

quote

TO DO

- _____
- _____
- _____
- _____
- _____
- _____
- _____
- _____
- _____
- _____

APPOINTMENTS-CALLS

NOTES

DAILY

DATE   __/__/____   FOCUS

quote

TO DO

- ○ _____
- ○ _____
- ○ _____
- ○ _____
- ○ _____
- ○ _____
- ○ _____
- ○ _____
- ○ _____
- ○ _____

APPOINTMENTS-CALLS

NOTES

Never let

YOUR FEAR DECIDE
YOUR FUTURE.

BILL PAYMENT TRACKER

BILL	DATE	$	JA	FB	MR	AP	MY	JN	JL	AG	SP	OC	NV	DE

SAVINGS TRACKER

FOR:

AMOUNT NEEDED:

DUE DATE	PLANNED	SAVED	STILL TO BE SAVED

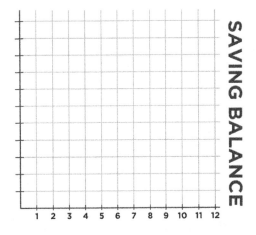

SAVING BALANCE

1 2 3 4 5 6 7 8 9 10 11 12

NOTES

MONTHLY BILLS

MONTH:	BUDGET GOAL:

INCOME

DATE	DESCRIPTION	AMOUNT	AFTER TAX

FIXED EXPENSES

DATE	DESCRIPTION	AMOUNT

OTHER EXPENSES

DATE	DESCRIPTION	AMOUNT

	BUDGETED	ACTUAL	DIFFERENCE
TOTAL EXPENSES			
TOTAL INCOME			
TOTAL SAVINGS			

DEBT PAYMENT TRACKER

DEBT:	CREDITOR:	PAYMENT DATE:

STARTING BALANCE: _____ **ACCOUNT:** _____

JANUARY	FEBRUARY	MARCH	APRIL	MAY	JUNE

JULY	AUGUST	SEPTEMBER	OCTOBER	NOVEMBER	DECEMBER

ENDING BALANCE: _____

DEBT:	CREDITOR:	PAYMENT DATE:

STARTING BALANCE: _____ **ACCOUNT:** _____

JANUARY	FEBRUARY	MARCH	APRIL	MAY	JUNE

JULY	AUGUST	SEPTEMBER	OCTOBER	NOVEMBER	DECEMBER

ENDING BALANCE: _____

DEBT:	CREDITOR:	PAYMENT DATE:

STARTING BALANCE: _____ **ACCOUNT:** _____

JANUARY	FEBRUARY	MARCH	APRIL	MAY	JUNE

JULY	AUGUST	SEPTEMBER	OCTOBER	NOVEMBER	DECEMBER

ENDING BALANCE: _____

MONTHLY BUDGET

ITEM	BUDGET	ACTUAL	DIFFERENCE	NOTES
CATEGORY:				
CATEGORY:				
CATEGORY:				
CATEGORY:				
CATEGORY:				

EXPENSE TRACKER

DATE	DESCRIPTION	INCOME	OUTGOING

TOTAL INCOME:	TOTAL OUTGOINGS:	BALANCE:

ACCOUNT DETAILS

ACCOUNT:	STARTING BALANCE:

DATE	TRANSACTION	WITHDRAWAL	DEPOSIT	BALANCE

NOTES

WEEKLY EXPENSES

ITEM	BUDGETED	ACTUAL	DIFFERENCE	DUE DATE	PAID
WEEK 1					

SAVINGS [ ] LEFTOVER [ ]

WEEK 2					

SAVINGS [ ] LEFTOVER [ ]

WEEKLY EXPENSES

ITEM	BUDGETED	ACTUAL	DIFFERENCE	DUE DATE	PAID
WEEK 3					

SAVINGS | LEFTOVER

ITEM	BUDGETED	ACTUAL	DIFFERENCE	DUE DATE	PAID
WEEK 4					

SAVINGS | LEFTOVER

MONTH: _____

TO DO LIST:

NOTES:

DAILY

DATE __/__/____   FOCUS

quote

TO DO

- ○ _____
- ○ _____
- ○ _____
- ○ _____
- ○ _____
- ○ _____
- ○ _____
- ○ _____
- ○ _____
- ○ _____

APPOINTMENTS-CALLS

NOTES

DAILY

DATE __/__/____   FOCUS

TO DO

○ _____
○ _____
○ _____
○ _____
○ _____
○ _____
○ _____
○ _____
○ _____
○ _____

APPOINTMENTS-CALLS

NOTES

DAILY

DATE __/__/____   FOCUS

quote

TO DO

○ _____
○ _____
○ _____
○ _____
○ _____
○ _____
○ _____
○ _____
○ _____
○ _____

APPOINTMENTS-CALLS

NOTES

DAILY

DATE __/__/____

FOCUS

TO DO

- ○ _____
- ○ _____
- ○ _____
- ○ _____
- ○ _____
- ○ _____
- ○ _____
- ○ _____
- ○ _____
- ○ _____

APPOINTMENTS-CALLS

NOTES

DAILY

DATE   __/__/____   FOCUS

quote

TO DO

- ○ _____
- ○ _____
- ○ _____
- ○ _____
- ○ _____
- ○ _____
- ○ _____
- ○ _____
- ○ _____
- ○ _____

APPOINTMENTS-CALLS

NOTES

The art of knowing

Is knowing what

TO IGNORE.

BILL PAYMENT TRACKER

BILL	DATE	$	JA	FB	MR	AP	MY	JN	JL	AG	SP	OC	NV	DE

SAVINGS TRACKER

FOR:	AMOUNT NEEDED:

DUE DATE	PLANNED	SAVED	STILL TO BE SAVED

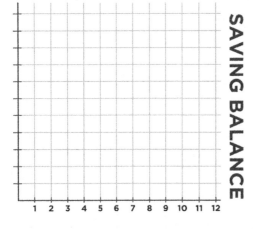

SAVING BALANCE

1 2 3 4 5 6 7 8 9 10 11 12

NOTES

MONTHLY BILLS

MONTH:	BUDGET GOAL:

INCOME

DATE	DESCRIPTION	AMOUNT	AFTER TAX

FIXED EXPENSES

DATE	DESCRIPTION	AMOUNT

OTHER EXPENSES

DATE	DESCRIPTION	AMOUNT

	BUDGETED	ACTUAL	DIFFERENCE
TOTAL EXPENSES			
TOTAL INCOME			
TOTAL SAVINGS			

DEBT PAYMENT TRACKER

DEBT:	CREDITOR:	PAYMENT DATE:

STARTING BALANCE: _____ **ACCOUNT:** _____

JANUARY	FEBRUARY	MARCH	APRIL	MAY	JUNE

JULY	AUGUST	SEPTEMBER	OCTOBER	NOVEMBER	DECEMBER

ENDING BALANCE: _____

DEBT:	CREDITOR:	PAYMENT DATE:

STARTING BALANCE: _____ **ACCOUNT:** _____

JANUARY	FEBRUARY	MARCH	APRIL	MAY	JUNE

JULY	AUGUST	SEPTEMBER	OCTOBER	NOVEMBER	DECEMBER

ENDING BALANCE: _____

DEBT:	CREDITOR:	PAYMENT DATE:

STARTING BALANCE: _____ **ACCOUNT:** _____

JANUARY	FEBRUARY	MARCH	APRIL	MAY	JUNE

JULY	AUGUST	SEPTEMBER	OCTOBER	NOVEMBER	DECEMBER

ENDING BALANCE: _____

MONTHLY BUDGET

ITEM	BUDGET	ACTUAL	DIFFERENCE	NOTES
CATEGORY:				
CATEGORY:				
CATEGORY:				
CATEGORY:				
CATEGORY:				

EXPENSE TRACKER

DATE	DESCRIPTION	INCOME	OUTGOING

TOTAL INCOME:	TOTAL OUTGOINGS:	BALANCE:

ACCOUNT DETAILS

ACCOUNT:	STARTING BALANCE:

DATE	TRANSACTION	WITHDRAWAL	DEPOSIT	BALANCE

NOTES

WEEKLY EXPENSES

ITEM	BUDGETED	ACTUAL	DIFFERENCE	DUE DATE	PAID
WEEK 1					

SAVINGS [   ]   LEFTOVER [   ]

ITEM	BUDGETED	ACTUAL	DIFFERENCE	DUE DATE	PAID
WEEK 2					

SAVINGS [   ]   LEFTOVER [   ]

WEEKLY EXPENSES

ITEM	BUDGETED	ACTUAL	DIFFERENCE	DUE DATE	PAID
WEEK 3					

SAVINGS [   ]   LEFTOVER [   ]

ITEM	BUDGETED	ACTUAL	DIFFERENCE	DUE DATE	PAID
WEEK 4					

SAVINGS [   ]   LEFTOVER [   ]

Be positive

MONTH: _____

TO DO LIST:

NOTES:

DAILY

DATE   __/__/____   FOCUS

quote

TO DO	APPOINTMENTS-CALLS
◯ _____	
◯ _____	
◯ _____	
◯ _____	
◯ _____	
◯ _____	
◯ _____	
◯ _____	
◯ _____	
◯ _____	

NOTES

DAILY

DATE __/__/____

FOCUS

TO DO

- ○ _____
- ○ _____
- ○ _____
- ○ _____
- ○ _____
- ○ _____
- ○ _____
- ○ _____
- ○ _____
- ○ _____

APPOINTMENTS-CALLS

NOTES

DAILY

DATE ___/___/_____ FOCUS

quote

TO DO

- _____
- _____
- _____
- _____
- _____
- _____
- _____
- _____
- _____
- _____

APPOINTMENTS-CALLS

NOTES

DAILY

DATE   __/__/____   FOCUS

quote

TO DO

○ _____
○ _____
○ _____
○ _____
○ _____
○ _____
○ _____
○ _____
○ _____
○ _____

APPOINTMENTS-CALLS

NOTES

DAILY

DATE __/__/____   FOCUS

(quote)

TO DO	APPOINTMENTS-CALLS
◯ _____	
◯ _____	
◯ _____	
◯ _____	
◯ _____	
◯ _____	
◯ _____	
◯ _____	
◯ _____	
◯ _____	

NOTES

BILL PAYMENT TRACKER

BILL	DATE	$	JA	FB	MR	AP	MY	JN	JL	AG	SP	OC	NV	DE

SAVINGS TRACKER

FOR:	AMOUNT NEEDED:

DUE DATE	PLANNED	SAVED	STILL TO BE SAVED

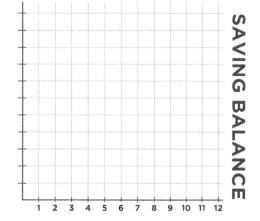

SAVING BALANCE

1 2 3 4 5 6 7 8 9 10 11 12

NOTES

MONTHLY BILLS

MONTH:	BUDGET GOAL:

INCOME

DATE	DESCRIPTION	AMOUNT	AFTER TAX

FIXED EXPENSES

DATE	DESCRIPTION	AMOUNT

OTHER EXPENSES

DATE	DESCRIPTION	AMOUNT

	BUDGETED	ACTUAL	DIFFERENCE
TOTAL EXPENSES			
TOTAL INCOME			
TOTAL SAVINGS			

DEBT PAYMENT TRACKER

DEBT: | **CREDITOR:** | **PAYMENT DATE:**

STARTING BALANCE: _____ **ACCOUNT:** _____

JANUARY	FEBRUARY	MARCH	APRIL	MAY	JUNE

JULY	AUGUST	SEPTEMBER	OCTOBER	NOVEMBER	DECEMBER

ENDING BALANCE: _____

DEBT: | **CREDITOR:** | **PAYMENT DATE:**

STARTING BALANCE: _____ **ACCOUNT:** _____

JANUARY	FEBRUARY	MARCH	APRIL	MAY	JUNE

JULY	AUGUST	SEPTEMBER	OCTOBER	NOVEMBER	DECEMBER

ENDING BALANCE: _____

DEBT: | **CREDITOR:** | **PAYMENT DATE:**

STARTING BALANCE: _____ **ACCOUNT:** _____

JANUARY	FEBRUARY	MARCH	APRIL	MAY	JUNE

JULY	AUGUST	SEPTEMBER	OCTOBER	NOVEMBER	DECEMBER

ENDING BALANCE: _____

MONTHLY BUDGET

ITEM	BUDGET	ACTUAL	DIFFERENCE	NOTES
CATEGORY:				
CATEGORY:				
CATEGORY:				
CATEGORY:				
CATEGORY:				

EXPENSE TRACKER

DATE	DESCRIPTION	INCOME	OUTGOING

TOTAL INCOME:	TOTAL OUTGOINGS:	BALANCE:

ACCOUNT DETAILS

ACCOUNT:

STARTING BALANCE:

DATE	TRANSACTION	WITHDRAWAL	DEPOSIT	BALANCE

NOTES

WEEKLY EXPENSES

ITEM	BUDGETED	ACTUAL	DIFFERENCE	DUE DATE	PAID
WEEK 1					

SAVINGS [　　　　　　　　]   LEFTOVER [　　　　　　　　]

ITEM	BUDGETED	ACTUAL	DIFFERENCE	DUE DATE	PAID
WEEK 2					

SAVINGS [　　　　　　　　]   LEFTOVER [　　　　　　　　]

WEEKLY EXPENSES

ITEM	BUDGETED	ACTUAL	DIFFERENCE	DUE DATE	PAID
WEEK 3					

SAVINGS _____   LEFTOVER _____

ITEM	BUDGETED	ACTUAL	DIFFERENCE	DUE DATE	PAID
WEEK 4					

SAVINGS _____   LEFTOVER _____

MONTH: _____

TO DO LIST:

NOTES:

DAILY

DATE __/__/____ FOCUS

quote

TO DO

○ _____
○ _____
○ _____
○ _____
○ _____
○ _____
○ _____
○ _____
○ _____
○ _____

APPOINTMENTS-CALLS

NOTES

DAILY

DATE __/__/____   FOCUS

TO DO

- ○ _____
- ○ _____
- ○ _____
- ○ _____
- ○ _____
- ○ _____
- ○ _____
- ○ _____
- ○ _____
- ○ _____

APPOINTMENTS-CALLS

NOTES

DAILY

DATE __/__/____ FOCUS

quote

TO DO

- ○ _____
- ○ _____
- ○ _____
- ○ _____
- ○ _____
- ○ _____
- ○ _____
- ○ _____
- ○ _____
- ○ _____

APPOINTMENTS-CALLS

NOTES

DAILY

DATE __/__/____   FOCUS

quote

TO DO

- ○ _____
- ○ _____
- ○ _____
- ○ _____
- ○ _____
- ○ _____
- ○ _____
- ○ _____
- ○ _____
- ○ _____

APPOINTMENTS-CALLS

NOTES

DAILY

DATE __/__/____   FOCUS

quote

TO DO

○ _____
○ _____
○ _____
○ _____
○ _____
○ _____
○ _____
○ _____
○ _____
○ _____

APPOINTMENTS-CALLS

NOTES

BILL PAYMENT TRACKER

BILL	DATE	$	JA	FB	MR	AP	MY	JN	JL	AG	SP	OC	NV	DE

SAVINGS TRACKER

FOR:	AMOUNT NEEDED:

DUE DATE	PLANNED	SAVED	STILL TO BE SAVED

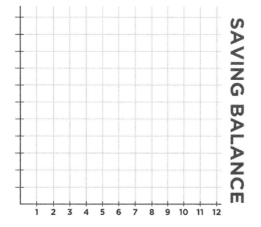

SAVING BALANCE

NOTES

MONTHLY BILLS

MONTH:	BUDGET GOAL:

INCOME

DATE	DESCRIPTION	AMOUNT	AFTER TAX

FIXED EXPENSES

DATE	DESCRIPTION	AMOUNT

OTHER EXPENSES

DATE	DESCRIPTION	AMOUNT

	BUDGETED	ACTUAL	DIFFERENCE
TOTAL EXPENSES			
TOTAL INCOME			
TOTAL SAVINGS			

DEBT PAYMENT TRACKER

DEBT:	CREDITOR:	PAYMENT DATE:

STARTING BALANCE: _____ **ACCOUNT:** _____

JANUARY	FEBRUARY	MARCH	APRIL	MAY	JUNE

JULY	AUGUST	SEPTEMBER	OCTOBER	NOVEMBER	DECEMBER

ENDING BALANCE: _____

DEBT:	CREDITOR:	PAYMENT DATE:

STARTING BALANCE: _____ **ACCOUNT:** _____

JANUARY	FEBRUARY	MARCH	APRIL	MAY	JUNE

JULY	AUGUST	SEPTEMBER	OCTOBER	NOVEMBER	DECEMBER

ENDING BALANCE: _____

DEBT:	CREDITOR:	PAYMENT DATE:

STARTING BALANCE: _____ **ACCOUNT:** _____

JANUARY	FEBRUARY	MARCH	APRIL	MAY	JUNE

JULY	AUGUST	SEPTEMBER	OCTOBER	NOVEMBER	DECEMBER

ENDING BALANCE: _____

MONTHLY BUDGET

ITEM	BUDGET	ACTUAL	DIFFERENCE	NOTES

CATEGORY:

CATEGORY:

CATEGORY:

CATEGORY:

CATEGORY:

EXPENSE TRACKER

DATE	DESCRIPTION	INCOME	OUTGOING

TOTAL INCOME:	TOTAL OUTGOINGS:	BALANCE:

ACCOUNT DETAILS

ACCOUNT:	STARTING BALANCE:

DATE	TRANSACTION	WITHDRAWAL	DEPOSIT	BALANCE

NOTES

WEEKLY EXPENSES

ITEM	BUDGETED	ACTUAL	DIFFERENCE	DUE DATE	PAID
WEEK 1					

SAVINGS [   ]   **LEFTOVER** [   ]

ITEM	BUDGETED	ACTUAL	DIFFERENCE	DUE DATE	PAID
WEEK 2					

SAVINGS [   ]   **LEFTOVER** [   ]

WEEKLY EXPENSES

ITEM	BUDGETED	ACTUAL	DIFFERENCE	DUE DATE	PAID
WEEK 3					

SAVINGS | | LEFTOVER | |

ITEM	BUDGETED	ACTUAL	DIFFERENCE	DUE DATE	PAID
WEEK 4					

SAVINGS | | LEFTOVER | |

MONTH: _____

TO DO LIST:

NOTES:

DAILY

DATE __/__/____   FOCUS

quote

TO DO	APPOINTMENTS-CALLS
○ _____	
○ _____	
○ _____	
○ _____	
○ _____	
○ _____	
○ _____	
○ _____	
○ _____	
○ _____	

NOTES

DAILY

DATE   __/__/____   FOCUS

TO DO

- ○ _____
- ○ _____
- ○ _____
- ○ _____
- ○ _____
- ○ _____
- ○ _____
- ○ _____
- ○ _____
- ○ _____

APPOINTMENTS-CALLS

NOTES

DAILY

quote

TO DO

- ○ _____
- ○ _____
- ○ _____
- ○ _____
- ○ _____
- ○ _____
- ○ _____
- ○ _____
- ○ _____
- ○ _____

APPOINTMENTS-CALLS

NOTES

DAILY

DATE   __/__/____   FOCUS

TO DO

- ○ _____
- ○ _____
- ○ _____
- ○ _____
- ○ _____
- ○ _____
- ○ _____
- ○ _____
- ○ _____
- ○ _____

APPOINTMENTS-CALLS

NOTES

DAILY

DATE __/__/____   FOCUS

quote

TO DO

○ _____
○ _____
○ _____
○ _____
○ _____
○ _____
○ _____
○ _____
○ _____
○ _____

APPOINTMENTS-CALLS

NOTES

DON'T EXPECT
To see a change
IF YOU DON'T
Make one

BILL PAYMENT TRACKER

BILL	DATE	$	JA	FB	MR	AP	MY	JN	JL	AG	SP	OC	NV	DE

SAVINGS TRACKER

FOR:	AMOUNT NEEDED:

DUE DATE	PLANNED	SAVED	STILL TO BE SAVED

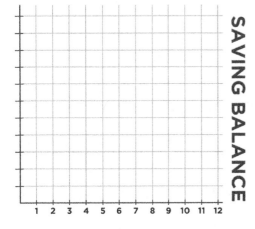

SAVING BALANCE

1 2 3 4 5 6 7 8 9 10 11 12

NOTES

MONTHLY BILLS

MONTH:	BUDGET GOAL:

INCOME

DATE	DESCRIPTION	AMOUNT	AFTER TAX

FIXED EXPENSES

DATE	DESCRIPTION	AMOUNT

OTHER EXPENSES

DATE	DESCRIPTION	AMOUNT

	BUDGETED	ACTUAL	DIFFERENCE
TOTAL EXPENSES			
TOTAL INCOME			
TOTAL SAVINGS			

DEBT PAYMENT TRACKER

DEBT:	CREDITOR:	PAYMENT DATE:

STARTING BALANCE: _____ **ACCOUNT:** _____

JANUARY	FEBRUARY	MARCH	APRIL	MAY	JUNE

JULY	AUGUST	SEPTEMBER	OCTOBER	NOVEMBER	DECEMBER

ENDING BALANCE: _____

DEBT:	CREDITOR:	PAYMENT DATE:

STARTING BALANCE: _____ **ACCOUNT:** _____

JANUARY	FEBRUARY	MARCH	APRIL	MAY	JUNE

JULY	AUGUST	SEPTEMBER	OCTOBER	NOVEMBER	DECEMBER

ENDING BALANCE: _____

DEBT:	CREDITOR:	PAYMENT DATE:

STARTING BALANCE: _____ **ACCOUNT:** _____

JANUARY	FEBRUARY	MARCH	APRIL	MAY	JUNE

JULY	AUGUST	SEPTEMBER	OCTOBER	NOVEMBER	DECEMBER

ENDING BALANCE: _____

MONTHLY BUDGET

ITEM	BUDGET	ACTUAL	DIFFERENCE	NOTES

CATEGORY:

CATEGORY:

CATEGORY:

CATEGORY:

CATEGORY:

EXPENSE TRACKER

DATE	DESCRIPTION	INCOME	OUTGOING

TOTAL INCOME:	TOTAL OUTGOINGS:	BALANCE:

ACCOUNT DETAILS

ACCOUNT:

STARTING BALANCE:

DATE	TRANSACTION	WITHDRAWAL	DEPOSIT	BALANCE

NOTES

WEEKLY EXPENSES

ITEM	BUDGETED	ACTUAL	DIFFERENCE	DUE DATE	PAID
WEEK 1					

SAVINGS [＿＿＿＿＿]   LEFTOVER [＿＿＿＿＿]

ITEM	BUDGETED	ACTUAL	DIFFERENCE	DUE DATE	PAID
WEEK 2					

SAVINGS [＿＿＿＿＿]   LEFTOVER [＿＿＿＿＿]

WEEKLY EXPENSES

ITEM	BUDGETED	ACTUAL	DIFFERENCE	DUE DATE	PAID
WEEK 3					

SAVINGS [ ]   LEFTOVER [ ]

ITEM	BUDGETED	ACTUAL	DIFFERENCE	DUE DATE	PAID
WEEK 4					

SAVINGS [ ]   LEFTOVER [ ]

We have tomorrows

for a reason.

MONTH: _____

TO DO LIST:

NOTES:

DAILY

DATE ___/___/_____   FOCUS

quote

TO DO

○ _____
○ _____
○ _____
○ _____
○ _____
○ _____
○ _____
○ _____
○ _____
○ _____

APPOINTMENTS-CALLS

NOTES

DAILY

DATE ___/___/_____   FOCUS

TO DO   APPOINTMENTS-CALLS

○ _____
○ _____
○ _____
○ _____
○ _____
○ _____
○ _____
○ _____
○ _____
○ _____

NOTES

DAILY

quote

TO DO

- ○ _____
- ○ _____
- ○ _____
- ○ _____
- ○ _____
- ○ _____
- ○ _____
- ○ _____
- ○ _____
- ○ _____

APPOINTMENTS-CALLS

NOTES

DAILY

DATE __/__/____

FOCUS

quote

TO DO

- ○ _____
- ○ _____
- ○ _____
- ○ _____
- ○ _____
- ○ _____
- ○ _____
- ○ _____
- ○ _____
- ○ _____

APPOINTMENTS-CALLS

NOTES

DAILY

DATE __/__/____   FOCUS

quote

TO DO

APPOINTMENTS-CALLS

○ _____
○ _____
○ _____
○ _____
○ _____
○ _____
○ _____
○ _____
○ _____
○ _____

NOTES

BILL PAYMENT TRACKER

BILL	DATE	$	JA	FB	MR	AP	MY	JN	JL	AG	SP	OC	NV	DE

SAVINGS TRACKER

FOR:	AMOUNT NEEDED:

DUE DATE	PLANNED	SAVED	STILL TO BE SAVED

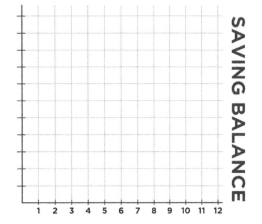

SAVING BALANCE

1 2 3 4 5 6 7 8 9 10 11 12

NOTES

MONTHLY BILLS

MONTH:	BUDGET GOAL:

INCOME

DATE	DESCRIPTION	AMOUNT	AFTER TAX

FIXED EXPENSES

DATE	DESCRIPTION	AMOUNT

OTHER EXPENSES

DATE	DESCRIPTION	AMOUNT

	BUDGETED	ACTUAL	DIFFERENCE
TOTAL EXPENSES			
TOTAL INCOME			
TOTAL SAVINGS			

DEBT PAYMENT TRACKER

DEBT:	CREDITOR:	PAYMENT DATE:

STARTING BALANCE: _____ ACCOUNT: _____

JANUARY	FEBRUARY	MARCH	APRIL	MAY	JUNE

JULY	AUGUST	SEPTEMBER	OCTOBER	NOVEMBER	DECEMBER

ENDING BALANCE: _____

DEBT:	CREDITOR:	PAYMENT DATE:

STARTING BALANCE: _____ ACCOUNT: _____

JANUARY	FEBRUARY	MARCH	APRIL	MAY	JUNE

JULY	AUGUST	SEPTEMBER	OCTOBER	NOVEMBER	DECEMBER

ENDING BALANCE: _____

DEBT:	CREDITOR:	PAYMENT DATE:

STARTING BALANCE: _____ ACCOUNT: _____

JANUARY	FEBRUARY	MARCH	APRIL	MAY	JUNE

JULY	AUGUST	SEPTEMBER	OCTOBER	NOVEMBER	DECEMBER

ENDING BALANCE: _____

MONTHLY BUDGET

ITEM	BUDGET	ACTUAL	DIFFERENCE	NOTES
CATEGORY:				
CATEGORY:				
CATEGORY:				
CATEGORY:				
CATEGORY:				

EXPENSE TRACKER

DATE	DESCRIPTION	INCOME	OUTGOING

TOTAL INCOME:	TOTAL OUTGOINGS:	BALANCE:

ACCOUNT DETAILS

ACCOUNT:		STARTING BALANCE:		

DATE	TRANSACTION	WITHDRAWAL	DEPOSIT	BALANCE

NOTES

WEEKLY EXPENSES

ITEM	BUDGETED	ACTUAL	DIFFERENCE	DUE DATE	PAID
WEEK 1					

SAVINGS [   ]   LEFTOVER [   ]

ITEM	BUDGETED	ACTUAL	DIFFERENCE	DUE DATE	PAID
WEEK 2					

SAVINGS [   ]   LEFTOVER [   ]

WEEKLY EXPENSES

ITEM	BUDGETED	ACTUAL	DIFFERENCE	DUE DATE	PAID
WEEK 3					

SAVINGS [   ]   LEFTOVER [   ]

ITEM	BUDGETED	ACTUAL	DIFFERENCE	DUE DATE	PAID
WEEK 4					

SAVINGS [   ]   LEFTOVER [   ]

MONTH: _____

NOTES:

DAILY

DATE __/__/____   FOCUS

quote

TO DO

APPOINTMENTS-CALLS

○ _____
○ _____
○ _____
○ _____
○ _____
○ _____
○ _____
○ _____
○ _____
○ _____

NOTES

DAILY

DATE   __/__/____   FOCUS

TO DO

- ○ _____
- ○ _____
- ○ _____
- ○ _____
- ○ _____
- ○ _____
- ○ _____
- ○ _____
- ○ _____
- ○ _____

APPOINTMENTS-CALLS

NOTES

DAILY

DATE __/__/____   FOCUS

quote

TO DO

○ _____

○ _____

○ _____

○ _____

○ _____

○ _____

○ _____

○ _____

○ _____

○ _____

APPOINTMENTS-CALLS

NOTES

DAILY

DATE __/__/____

FOCUS

quote

TO DO

APPOINTMENTS-CALLS

○ _____
○ _____
○ _____
○ _____
○ _____
○ _____
○ _____
○ _____
○ _____
○ _____

NOTES

DAILY

DATE   __/__/____   FOCUS

quote

TO DO

○ _____

○ _____

○ _____

○ _____

○ _____

○ _____

○ _____

○ _____

○ _____

○ _____

APPOINTMENTS-CALLS

NOTES

I CAN
AND
I WILL

BILL PAYMENT TRACKER

BILL	DATE	$	JA	FB	MR	AP	MY	JN	JL	AG	SP	OC	NV	DE

SAVINGS TRACKER

FOR:	AMOUNT NEEDED:

DUE DATE	PLANNED	SAVED	STILL TO BE SAVED

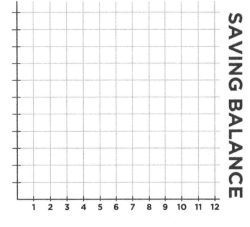

SAVING BALANCE

1 2 3 4 5 6 7 8 9 10 11 12

NOTES

MONTHLY BILLS

MONTH:	BUDGET GOAL:

INCOME

DATE	DESCRIPTION	AMOUNT	AFTER TAX

FIXED EXPENSES

DATE	DESCRIPTION	AMOUNT

OTHER EXPENSES

DATE	DESCRIPTION	AMOUNT

	BUDGETED	ACTUAL	DIFFERENCE
TOTAL EXPENSES			
TOTAL INCOME			
TOTAL SAVINGS			

DEBT PAYMENT TRACKER

DEBT:	CREDITOR:	PAYMENT DATE:

STARTING BALANCE: _____ **ACCOUNT:** _____

JANUARY	FEBRUARY	MARCH	APRIL	MAY	JUNE

JULY	AUGUST	SEPTEMBER	OCTOBER	NOVEMBER	DECEMBER

ENDING BALANCE: _____

DEBT:	CREDITOR:	PAYMENT DATE:

STARTING BALANCE: _____ **ACCOUNT:** _____

JANUARY	FEBRUARY	MARCH	APRIL	MAY	JUNE

JULY	AUGUST	SEPTEMBER	OCTOBER	NOVEMBER	DECEMBER

ENDING BALANCE: _____

DEBT:	CREDITOR:	PAYMENT DATE:

STARTING BALANCE: _____ **ACCOUNT:** _____

JANUARY	FEBRUARY	MARCH	APRIL	MAY	JUNE

JULY	AUGUST	SEPTEMBER	OCTOBER	NOVEMBER	DECEMBER

ENDING BALANCE: _____

MONTHLY BUDGET

ITEM	BUDGET	ACTUAL	DIFFERENCE	NOTES
CATEGORY:				
CATEGORY:				
CATEGORY:				
CATEGORY:				
CATEGORY:				

EXPENSE TRACKER

DATE	DESCRIPTION	INCOME	OUTGOING

TOTAL INCOME:	TOTAL OUTGOINGS:	BALANCE:

ACCOUNT DETAILS

ACCOUNT:		STARTING BALANCE:		

DATE	TRANSACTION	WITHDRAWAL	DEPOSIT	BALANCE

NOTES

WEEKLY EXPENSES

ITEM	BUDGETED	ACTUAL	DIFFERENCE	DUE DATE	PAID
WEEK 1					

SAVINGS [   ]   LEFTOVER [   ]

ITEM	BUDGETED	ACTUAL	DIFFERENCE	DUE DATE	PAID
WEEK 2					

SAVINGS [   ]   LEFTOVER [   ]

WEEKLY EXPENSES

ITEM	BUDGETED	ACTUAL	DIFFERENCE	DUE DATE	PAID
WEEK 3					
SAVINGS			**LEFTOVER**		
WEEK 4					
SAVINGS			**LEFTOVER**		

MONTH: _____

TO DO LIST:

NOTES:

DAILY

DATE __/__/____   FOCUS

quote

TO DO

○ _____
○ _____
○ _____
○ _____
○ _____
○ _____
○ _____
○ _____
○ _____
○ _____

APPOINTMENTS-CALLS

NOTES

DAILY

DATE __/__/____

FOCUS

TO DO

- ○ _____
- ○ _____
- ○ _____
- ○ _____
- ○ _____
- ○ _____
- ○ _____
- ○ _____
- ○ _____
- ○ _____

APPOINTMENTS-CALLS

NOTES

DAILY

DATE __/__/____   FOCUS

quote

TO DO

○ _____
○ _____
○ _____
○ _____
○ _____
○ _____
○ _____
○ _____
○ _____
○ _____

APPOINTMENTS-CALLS

NOTES

DAILY

DATE __/__/____

FOCUS

quote

TO DO

- _____
- _____
- _____
- _____
- _____
- _____
- _____
- _____
- _____
- _____

APPOINTMENTS-CALLS

NOTES

DAILY

DATE   __/__/____   FOCUS

(quote)

TO DO

APPOINTMENTS-CALLS

- ○ _____
- ○ _____
- ○ _____
- ○ _____
- ○ _____
- ○ _____
- ○ _____
- ○ _____
- ○ _____
- ○ _____

NOTES

BILL PAYMENT TRACKER

BILL	DATE	$	JA	FB	MR	AP	MY	JN	JL	AG	SP	OC	NV	DE

SAVINGS TRACKER

FOR:	AMOUNT NEEDED:

DUE DATE	PLANNED	SAVED	STILL TO BE SAVED

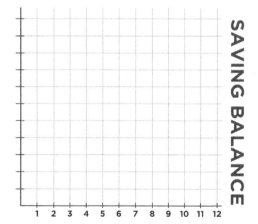

SAVING BALANCE

1 2 3 4 5 6 7 8 9 10 11 12

NOTES

MONTHLY BILLS

MONTH:	BUDGET GOAL:

INCOME			
DATE	DESCRIPTION	AMOUNT	AFTER TAX

FIXED EXPENSES			OTHER EXPENSES		
DATE	DESCRIPTION	AMOUNT	DATE	DESCRIPTION	AMOUNT

	BUDGETED	ACTUAL	DIFFERENCE
TOTAL EXPENSES			
TOTAL INCOME			
TOTAL SAVINGS			

DEBT PAYMENT TRACKER

DEBT:	CREDITOR:	PAYMENT DATE:

STARTING BALANCE: _____ **ACCOUNT:** _____

JANUARY	FEBRUARY	MARCH	APRIL	MAY	JUNE

JULY	AUGUST	SEPTEMBER	OCTOBER	NOVEMBER	DECEMBER

ENDING BALANCE: _____

DEBT:	CREDITOR:	PAYMENT DATE:

STARTING BALANCE: _____ **ACCOUNT:** _____

JANUARY	FEBRUARY	MARCH	APRIL	MAY	JUNE

JULY	AUGUST	SEPTEMBER	OCTOBER	NOVEMBER	DECEMBER

ENDING BALANCE: _____

DEBT:	CREDITOR:	PAYMENT DATE:

STARTING BALANCE: _____ **ACCOUNT:** _____

JANUARY	FEBRUARY	MARCH	APRIL	MAY	JUNE

JULY	AUGUST	SEPTEMBER	OCTOBER	NOVEMBER	DECEMBER

ENDING BALANCE: _____

MONTHLY BUDGET

ITEM	BUDGET	ACTUAL	DIFFERENCE	NOTES
CATEGORY:				
CATEGORY:				
CATEGORY:				
CATEGORY:				
CATEGORY:				

EXPENSE TRACKER

DATE	DESCRIPTION	INCOME	OUTGOING

TOTAL INCOME:	TOTAL OUTGOINGS:	BALANCE:

ACCOUNT DETAILS

ACCOUNT:

STARTING BALANCE:

DATE	TRANSACTION	WITHDRAWAL	DEPOSIT	BALANCE

NOTES

WEEKLY EXPENSES

ITEM	BUDGETED	ACTUAL	DIFFERENCE	DUE DATE	PAID
WEEK 1					

SAVINGS _____ **LEFTOVER** _____

ITEM	BUDGETED	ACTUAL	DIFFERENCE	DUE DATE	PAID
WEEK 2					

SAVINGS _____ **LEFTOVER** _____

WEEKLY EXPENSES

ITEM	BUDGETED	ACTUAL	DIFFERENCE	DUE DATE	PAID
WEEK 3					

SAVINGS [   ]   LEFTOVER [   ]

ITEM	BUDGETED	ACTUAL	DIFFERENCE	DUE DATE	PAID
WEEK 4					

SAVINGS [   ]   LEFTOVER [   ]

MONTH: _____

TO DO LIST:

NOTES:

DAILY

DATE __/__/____   FOCUS

quote

TO DO

○ _____
○ _____
○ _____
○ _____
○ _____
○ _____
○ _____
○ _____
○ _____
○ _____

APPOINTMENTS-CALLS

NOTES

DAILY

DATE __/__/____   FOCUS

quote

TO DO

○ _____
○ _____
○ _____
○ _____
○ _____
○ _____
○ _____
○ _____
○ _____
○ _____

APPOINTMENTS-CALLS

NOTES

DAILY

DATE ___/___/_____   FOCUS

quote

TO DO

○ _____
○ _____
○ _____
○ _____
○ _____
○ _____
○ _____
○ _____
○ _____
○ _____

APPOINTMENTS-CALLS

NOTES

DAILY

DATE __/__/____

FOCUS

quote

TO DO

○ _____
○ _____
○ _____
○ _____
○ _____
○ _____
○ _____
○ _____
○ _____
○ _____

APPOINTMENTS-CALLS

NOTES

DAILY

DATE __/__/____   FOCUS

quote

TO DO	APPOINTMENTS-CALLS
○ _____	
○ _____	
○ _____	
○ _____	
○ _____	
○ _____	
○ _____	
○ _____	
○ _____	
○ _____	

NOTES

Make it happen
shock everyone

BILL PAYMENT TRACKER

BILL	DATE	$	JA	FB	MR	AP	MY	JN	JL	AG	SP	OC	NV	DE

SAVINGS TRACKER

FOR:	AMOUNT NEEDED:

DUE DATE	PLANNED	SAVED	STILL TO BE SAVED

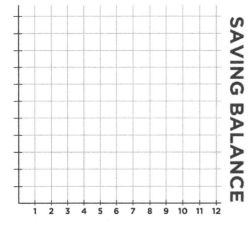

SAVING BALANCE

1 2 3 4 5 6 7 8 9 10 11 12

NOTES

MONTHLY BILLS

MONTH:		BUDGET GOAL:	

INCOME

DATE	DESCRIPTION	AMOUNT	AFTER TAX

FIXED EXPENSES

DATE	DESCRIPTION	AMOUNT

OTHER EXPENSES

DATE	DESCRIPTION	AMOUNT

	BUDGETED	ACTUAL	DIFFERENCE
TOTAL EXPENSES			
TOTAL INCOME			
TOTAL SAVINGS			

DEBT PAYMENT TRACKER

DEBT:	CREDITOR:	PAYMENT DATE:

STARTING BALANCE: _____ **ACCOUNT:** _____

JANUARY	FEBRUARY	MARCH	APRIL	MAY	JUNE

JULY	AUGUST	SEPTEMBER	OCTOBER	NOVEMBER	DECEMBER

ENDING BALANCE: _____

DEBT:	CREDITOR:	PAYMENT DATE:

STARTING BALANCE: _____ **ACCOUNT:** _____

JANUARY	FEBRUARY	MARCH	APRIL	MAY	JUNE

JULY	AUGUST	SEPTEMBER	OCTOBER	NOVEMBER	DECEMBER

ENDING BALANCE: _____

DEBT:	CREDITOR:	PAYMENT DATE:

STARTING BALANCE: _____ **ACCOUNT:** _____

JANUARY	FEBRUARY	MARCH	APRIL	MAY	JUNE

JULY	AUGUST	SEPTEMBER	OCTOBER	NOVEMBER	DECEMBER

ENDING BALANCE: _____

MONTHLY BUDGET

ITEM	BUDGET	ACTUAL	DIFFERENCE	NOTES
CATEGORY:				
CATEGORY:				
CATEGORY:				
CATEGORY:				
CATEGORY:				

EXPENSE TRACKER

DATE	DESCRIPTION	INCOME	OUTGOING

TOTAL INCOME:	TOTAL OUTGOINGS:	BALANCE:

ACCOUNT DETAILS

ACCOUNT:	STARTING BALANCE:

DATE	TRANSACTION	WITHDRAWAL	DEPOSIT	BALANCE

NOTES

WEEKLY EXPENSES

ITEM	BUDGETED	ACTUAL	DIFFERENCE	DUE DATE	PAID
WEEK 1					

SAVINGS [   ]   LEFTOVER [   ]

ITEM	BUDGETED	ACTUAL	DIFFERENCE	DUE DATE	PAID
WEEK 2					

SAVINGS [   ]   LEFTOVER [   ]

WEEKLY EXPENSES

ITEM	BUDGETED	ACTUAL	DIFFERENCE	DUE DATE	PAID
WEEK 3					

SAVINGS [   ]   LEFTOVER [   ]

ITEM	BUDGETED	ACTUAL	DIFFERENCE	DUE DATE	PAID
WEEK 4					

SAVINGS [   ]   LEFTOVER [   ]

LIVE BOLDLY.
PUSH YOURSELF.
DON'T SETTLE.

MONTH: _____

TO DO LIST:

NOTES:

DAILY

DATE __/__/____ FOCUS

quote

TO DO

APPOINTMENTS-CALLS

○ _____
○ _____
○ _____
○ _____
○ _____
○ _____
○ _____
○ _____
○ _____
○ _____

NOTES

DAILY

DATE __/__/____   FOCUS

TO DO

- ○ _____
- ○ _____
- ○ _____
- ○ _____
- ○ _____
- ○ _____
- ○ _____
- ○ _____
- ○ _____
- ○ _____

APPOINTMENTS-CALLS

NOTES

DAILY

DATE ___/___/_____   FOCUS

quote

TO DO

- ○ _____
- ○ _____
- ○ _____
- ○ _____
- ○ _____
- ○ _____
- ○ _____
- ○ _____
- ○ _____
- ○ _____

APPOINTMENTS-CALLS

NOTES

DAILY

DATE __/__/____

FOCUS

TO DO

○ _____
○ _____
○ _____
○ _____
○ _____
○ _____
○ _____
○ _____
○ _____
○ _____

APPOINTMENTS-CALLS

NOTES

DAILY

DATE   __/__/____   FOCUS

quote

TO DO

- ○ _____
- ○ _____
- ○ _____
- ○ _____
- ○ _____
- ○ _____
- ○ _____
- ○ _____
- ○ _____
- ○ _____

APPOINTMENTS-CALLS

NOTES

BILL PAYMENT TRACKER

BILL	DATE	$	JA	FB	MR	AP	MY	JN	JL	AG	SP	OC	NV	DE

SAVINGS TRACKER

FOR:	AMOUNT NEEDED:

DUE DATE	PLANNED	SAVED	STILL TO BE SAVED

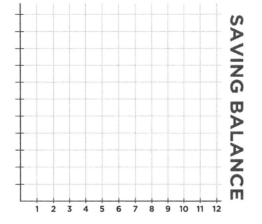

SAVING BALANCE

1 2 3 4 5 6 7 8 9 10 11 12

NOTES

MONTHLY BILLS

MONTH:	BUDGET GOAL:

INCOME

DATE	DESCRIPTION	AMOUNT	AFTER TAX

FIXED EXPENSES

DATE	DESCRIPTION	AMOUNT

OTHER EXPENSES

DATE	DESCRIPTION	AMOUNT

	BUDGETED	ACTUAL	DIFFERENCE
TOTAL EXPENSES			
TOTAL INCOME			
TOTAL SAVINGS			

DEBT PAYMENT TRACKER

DEBT:	CREDITOR:	PAYMENT DATE:

STARTING BALANCE: _____ **ACCOUNT:** _____

JANUARY	FEBRUARY	MARCH	APRIL	MAY	JUNE

JULY	AUGUST	SEPTEMBER	OCTOBER	NOVEMBER	DECEMBER

ENDING BALANCE: _____

DEBT:	CREDITOR:	PAYMENT DATE:

STARTING BALANCE: _____ **ACCOUNT:** _____

JANUARY	FEBRUARY	MARCH	APRIL	MAY	JUNE

JULY	AUGUST	SEPTEMBER	OCTOBER	NOVEMBER	DECEMBER

ENDING BALANCE: _____

DEBT:	CREDITOR:	PAYMENT DATE:

STARTING BALANCE: _____ **ACCOUNT:** _____

JANUARY	FEBRUARY	MARCH	APRIL	MAY	JUNE

JULY	AUGUST	SEPTEMBER	OCTOBER	NOVEMBER	DECEMBER

ENDING BALANCE: _____

MONTHLY BUDGET

ITEM	BUDGET	ACTUAL	DIFFERENCE	NOTES
CATEGORY:				
CATEGORY:				
CATEGORY:				
CATEGORY:				
CATEGORY:				

EXPENSE TRACKER

DATE	DESCRIPTION	INCOME	OUTGOING

TOTAL INCOME:	TOTAL OUTGOINGS:	BALANCE:

ACCOUNT DETAILS

ACCOUNT:

STARTING BALANCE:

DATE	TRANSACTION	WITHDRAWAL	DEPOSIT	BALANCE

NOTES

WEEKLY EXPENSES

ITEM	BUDGETED	ACTUAL	DIFFERENCE	DUE DATE	PAID
WEEK 1					

SAVINGS [＿＿＿＿＿＿]　　　　LEFTOVER [＿＿＿＿＿＿]

ITEM	BUDGETED	ACTUAL	DIFFERENCE	DUE DATE	PAID
WEEK 2					

SAVINGS [＿＿＿＿＿＿]　　　　LEFTOVER [＿＿＿＿＿＿]

WEEKLY EXPENSES

ITEM	BUDGETED	ACTUAL	DIFFERENCE	DUE DATE	PAID
WEEK 3					

SAVINGS [   ]   LEFTOVER [   ]

ITEM	BUDGETED	ACTUAL	DIFFERENCE	DUE DATE	PAID
WEEK 4					

SAVINGS [   ]   LEFTOVER [   ]

MONTH: _____

TO DO LIST:

NOTES:

DAILY

DATE __/__/____   FOCUS

quote

TO DO   APPOINTMENTS-CALLS

○ _____
○ _____
○ _____
○ _____
○ _____
○ _____
○ _____
○ _____
○ _____
○ _____

NOTES

DAILY

DATE   __/__/____

FOCUS

quote

TO DO

- _____
- _____
- _____
- _____
- _____
- _____
- _____
- _____
- _____
- _____

APPOINTMENTS-CALLS

NOTES

DAILY

DATE __/__/____   FOCUS

quote

TO DO

○ _____

○ _____

○ _____

○ _____

○ _____

○ _____

○ _____

○ _____

○ _____

○ _____

APPOINTMENTS-CALLS

NOTES

DAILY

DATE __/__/____   FOCUS

TO DO

- ○ _____
- ○ _____
- ○ _____
- ○ _____
- ○ _____
- ○ _____
- ○ _____
- ○ _____
- ○ _____
- ○ _____

APPOINTMENTS-CALLS

NOTES

DAILY

DATE   __/__/____   FOCUS

quote

TO DO

○ _____

○ _____

○ _____

○ _____

○ _____

○ _____

○ _____

○ _____

○ _____

○ _____

APPOINTMENTS-CALLS

NOTES

The simple things

in

Life

BILL PAYMENT TRACKER

BILL	DATE	$	JA	FB	MR	AP	MY	JN	JL	AG	SP	OC	NV	DE

SAVINGS TRACKER

FOR:	AMOUNT NEEDED:

DUE DATE	PLANNED	SAVED	STILL TO BE SAVED

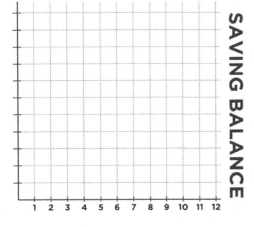

SAVING BALANCE

1 2 3 4 5 6 7 8 9 10 11 12

NOTES

MONTHLY BILLS

MONTH:	BUDGET GOAL:

INCOME

DATE	DESCRIPTION	AMOUNT	AFTER TAX

FIXED EXPENSES

DATE	DESCRIPTION	AMOUNT

OTHER EXPENSES

DATE	DESCRIPTION	AMOUNT

	BUDGETED	ACTUAL	DIFFERENCE
TOTAL EXPENSES			
TOTAL INCOME			
TOTAL SAVINGS			

DEBT PAYMENT TRACKER

DEBT:	CREDITOR:	PAYMENT DATE:

STARTING BALANCE: _____ ACCOUNT: _____

JANUARY	FEBRUARY	MARCH	APRIL	MAY	JUNE

JULY	AUGUST	SEPTEMBER	OCTOBER	NOVEMBER	DECEMBER

ENDING BALANCE: _____

DEBT:	CREDITOR:	PAYMENT DATE:

STARTING BALANCE: _____ ACCOUNT: _____

JANUARY	FEBRUARY	MARCH	APRIL	MAY	JUNE

JULY	AUGUST	SEPTEMBER	OCTOBER	NOVEMBER	DECEMBER

ENDING BALANCE: _____

DEBT:	CREDITOR:	PAYMENT DATE:

STARTING BALANCE: _____ ACCOUNT: _____

JANUARY	FEBRUARY	MARCH	APRIL	MAY	JUNE

JULY	AUGUST	SEPTEMBER	OCTOBER	NOVEMBER	DECEMBER

ENDING BALANCE: _____

MONTHLY BUDGET

ITEM	BUDGET	ACTUAL	DIFFERENCE	NOTES
CATEGORY:				
CATEGORY:				
CATEGORY:				
CATEGORY:				
CATEGORY:				

EXPENSE TRACKER

DATE	DESCRIPTION	INCOME	OUTGOING

TOTAL INCOME:	TOTAL OUTGOINGS:	BALANCE:

ACCOUNT DETAILS

ACCOUNT:

STARTING BALANCE:

DATE	TRANSACTION	WITHDRAWAL	DEPOSIT	BALANCE

NOTES

WEEKLY EXPENSES

ITEM	BUDGETED	ACTUAL	DIFFERENCE	DUE DATE	PAID
WEEK 1					

SAVINGS [　　　　　]   **LEFTOVER** [　　　　　]

ITEM	BUDGETED	ACTUAL	DIFFERENCE	DUE DATE	PAID
WEEK 2					

SAVINGS [　　　　　]   **LEFTOVER** [　　　　　]

WEEKLY EXPENSES

ITEM	BUDGETED	ACTUAL	DIFFERENCE	DUE DATE	PAID
WEEK 3					

SAVINGS [＿＿＿＿＿＿]   LEFTOVER [＿＿＿＿＿＿]

ITEM	BUDGETED	ACTUAL	DIFFERENCE	DUE DATE	PAID
WEEK 4					

SAVINGS [＿＿＿＿＿＿]   LEFTOVER [＿＿＿＿＿＿]

MONTH: _____

TO DO LIST:

NOTES:

DAILY

DATE __/__/____   FOCUS

quote

TO DO

○ _____
○ _____
○ _____
○ _____
○ _____
○ _____
○ _____
○ _____
○ _____
○ _____

APPOINTMENTS-CALLS

NOTES

DAILY

DATE ___/___/_____

FOCUS

quote

TO DO

APPOINTMENTS-CALLS

- ○ _____
- ○ _____
- ○ _____
- ○ _____
- ○ _____
- ○ _____
- ○ _____
- ○ _____
- ○ _____
- ○ _____

NOTES

DAILY

DATE ___/___/_____   FOCUS

quote

TO DO	APPOINTMENTS-CALLS

○ _____
○ _____
○ _____
○ _____
○ _____
○ _____
○ _____
○ _____
○ _____
○ _____

NOTES

DAILY

DATE __/__/____   FOCUS

(quote)

TO DO

- ○ _____
- ○ _____
- ○ _____
- ○ _____
- ○ _____
- ○ _____
- ○ _____
- ○ _____
- ○ _____
- ○ _____

APPOINTMENTS-CALLS

NOTES

DAILY

DATE   __/__/____   FOCUS

quote

TO DO

- ○ _____
- ○ _____
- ○ _____
- ○ _____
- ○ _____
- ○ _____
- ○ _____
- ○ _____
- ○ _____
- ○ _____

APPOINTMENTS-CALLS

NOTES

NOTES

NOTES

NOTES

NOTES

NOTES

NOTES

NOTES

NOTES

NOTES

NOTES

NOTES

NOTES

NOTES

NOTES

NOTES

NOTES

Made in the USA
Las Vegas, NV
06 May 2023

71680201R00125